THE HUNTER'S CREED

A great primer for new hunters and
a good refresher for seasoned hunters

includes bonus *Concepts for Survival* handbook

by Garn G. Christensen

"he moves with quiet speed
alone through the night
watching and waiting"

"the lonely call searching for the others"

In memory of Ural Latham

Garn Christensen served as a licensed Outfitter and Guide in the River of No Return Wilderness area, located in the heart of Idaho. Garn has over forty years of hunting and fishing experience. His concepts on hunting ethics and survival skills have been presented in national publications as well as on commercial television and public radio.

Janis Wheeler is a successful traditional archer. She has been the graphic design director of *Traditional Bow Hunter Magazine* and a contributing artist for the Craters of the Moon National Monument.

Janis has painted and drawn wildlife and takes upon her experience as a sportswoman and her love of the outdoors to give her the inspiration for her work. In her illustrations for this book, Janis hopes to portray just some of the abundant wildlife we all have to enjoy.

I dedicate The Hunters Creed to my children: Kelly, Buck, James, Aireus, Skylar, Anthea, and my grandchildren: Abram, Anna, Riley, Aubrie, Tasya, Megan, Jessica, Hazen, Ian, Jacob, Eliza, Morgan, Nicolas, Isaac, Bristol, Camas, Tilda, Onyx, Augustine & Elias, and all of my great-grandchildren.

ACKNOWLEDGEMENTS

My special thanks to my wife Jackie for her support. To Diana Schulz for helping me get these words in print. To Janis Wheeler for her faith and talent as an illustrator. To Mary Jane Oresik of DTP TEAM for her diligence in composing my materials and to Matt Cantrill for his help with the revisions.

"sun, fire...
water, healing...
air, earth, new life...
we are the caretakers"

FORWARD

Several years ago I took my oldest grandson, Abram, on his first fishing trip. As we fished together, he started asking questions that were basic to man's relationship with wildlife. The answers I gave Abram were not new, but rather echoes of words which I had received from my father and grandfather. That old wisdom had been a part of my life for many years, however to Abram, the information was new and exciting. Our conversation moved from fishing to hunting, and as we talked I thought how often I have met fishermen and hunters with virtually no basic knowledge of ethics or skills. Their lack of this vital information not only reduced their success in the field, but of more importance, often unnecessarily harmed wildlife, and frequently resulted in trouble with the law.

I feel strongly that hunting is much more than just killing. With this belief, my desire in writing **The Hunter's Creed** is to pass on to my grandchildren, as well as future generations of hunters and fishermen, some of this old knowledge which may help them make intelligent and honorable decisions in the field.

I am part of this beautiful earth and will strive to understand, respect and protect its wonders. I will always walk gently so as to leave the wilderness as it was before I touched it.

I think of the Earth in the terms of the North American Indians. They feel the Earth is their loving and nurturing Grandmother, therefore, it is difficult to cause her harm. The skill of hunting and living in the wilderness can only be gained through experience. Learn to be silent and observant. Understand that the Earth is friendly.

The Native Americans had a special sense of living on this Earth and created the symbols of the medicine wheel to express this understanding. The direction of the Earth on the medicine wheel is the South. The Dakota's portrayed the South as green and the Cheyenne used the color white.

The mouse is often the animal associated with the South or the Earth. The lesson of the mouse is that it sees a limited view of the world. Living closely to the ground, it does not experience the vision of the eagle, yet every gift it needs in life is provided within the circle of its existence.

The Earth offers other gifts including innocence, honesty, touching, and new life or beginning. All are good lessons to understand as you live with the Grandmother.

Deer hunting was the means by which our family acquired its winter supply of meat. Our large hunting parties were all family members, many of whom had hunted together since the long past days of their youth.

I remember the first year that I, a youth of fourteen, was permitted to carry a rifle. In preparation for the hunt, I had spent days cleaning and sighting in the WWII German Mauser. We were hunting at the base of Mount Nebo. The camp was made up of two wall tents for sleeping and an old army medical tent we used for cooking. The camp was at the bottom of three large drainage, all of which had big herds of mule deer. The hunters were all my uncles, cousins or brothers and the party had members ranging in age from eight to seventy nine. The camp was tight, dry and warm.

It was early on the opening morning of the hunt when my brother, Dan, and I left camp in a full force blizzard and started up a steep and narrow canyon. The top of the ridges would offer the best point from which to observe the drive that would come up from the bottom. John Roberts and his sons would hunt their way up the brush filled canyon pushing deer up to a ridge where we would be watching. Hunting drives were a way of hunting a large area for our family, and we had used this technique for years. I felt proud in being assigned to head off the drive, rather than being with the hunters pushing the animals. You had to be a true shot, with keen eyes to get to be the trap hunter. The fact that it was the first year that I carried a rifle may have influenced my family to give me a good opportunity to use it. We separated and moved up each side of the canyon. Visibility was limited to about twenty feet and climbing was very rough, but I finally reached a ledge just below the ridge line. Through the dim light and heavy snow, I could just barely make out the well used game trail fifty feet below my position. I tucked myself into a crevice in a large rock outcropping and tried not to think about the bitter cold. The trail faded in and out as burst of driven snow obscured my view. Finally, the wind stopped and the snow lightened to flakes the size of silver half dollars. I looked across the canyon to see if I could spot my brother. I could not, and turned my eyes back to the trail. As the blowing let up, my vision seemed to go through a soft focusing and on the trail below I saw a large four point buck. Instantly, my heart began to pound and I stopped breathing. Just as I brought my rifle up and peered through the peep sight, a movement in front of the buck caught my attention. It was another big buck, just ahead of the four point. Three more bucks followed the four point. Never before had I felt such a surge of adrenaline. I sighted, pushed the safety off, squeezed the trigger, pulled the bolt back to eject the spent shell, slid the bolt forward, chambering the next round, sighted, pulled the trigger, ejected the shell, repeating the action over and over until all five shots were fired. I looked down on the trail. My senses were overloaded and going in a thousand directions at the same instant. On the trail lay two dead and two dying deer. The four point and a large three point were dead. The fork horn and small four point were still moving. I climbed down to the trail near the four point. Shocked by what I had done, I felt fear and cold numbness. I shall never forget the pleading, hurt eyes of those wounded deer. I cut each deer's throat then, in a daze, headed down the canyon.

As I neared camp, it began snowing hard again. My brother and three others were near the stove drinking coffee when I went into the tent, tears streaming down my face. The blizzard had forced them back to camp.

"My God, whats wrong?" Dan demanded. I told him I had done something horrible. My brother calmed me down and I told him what had happened. Not only was I overwhelmed by that first killing but I was also concerned about the game laws I had broken.

Dan and I went back into the canyon, cleaned the deer and packed them out. The storm grew much worse and only one other deer was taken. The group of twelve hunters shared the meat.

Dan later told me that judging from my appearance and emotional state, he thought I had killed someone. In retrospect, he was right. I had killed a part within myself that had never taken a life and could never return to that point of innocence and naivete again.

It is no longer a necessity for me to take a deer for winter meat, yet I would not hesitate to kill a deer or elk if my family were in genuine need of food. I am a hunter; and will teach my children to hunt if they desire, just as I was taught by my father and his father. Hunting sustains life with more than meat. Hunting is a strong instinct and ancient impulse that comes from deep within.

Before taking a life, consider well all your reasons, as it will be an action you will always recall.

"strength,
perseverance,
endurance"

I know that the taking of an animal's life is a powerful action and must be accomplished with respect and thoughtfulness.

I value wildlife and always eat what I kill. In survival courses, that I have instructed, one of the first lessons that I teach is that what you kill you eat. During a course conducted for a group of foster kids, a young boy, Carl, made a throwing stick, a tool used by many tribes to dig roots and kill small game such as rabbits and birds. Skillfully thrown, it whirls through the air like the rotor blades on a helicopter. I had shown the group how to use the stick and Carl was using a log for target practice when a ground squirrel ventured near the log. He let the stick fly at the squirrel and hit it. Carl was shocked when it fell dead. Together we went to the animal and discussed what he had just done. He had never killed anything and was confused by his action.

I told him that what he had done was right, as we needed the meat for the evening meal. I suggested he give thanks for the life of the squirrel and make good use of its meat and skin. He helped me cook it and later made a small medicine bag from the skin. Years later, Carl told me that killing the squirrel was one of the most profound moments in his life. The action gave him valuable insight, and he still has the medicine bag.

I know that the only moral purpose for taking an animal's life is to sustain life.

"an act...done unthinking
can never be undone"

**I will study in detail the animals that I
hunt. I will know them as living
animals in their environment before**

taking their life.

In the fall of 1976 my wife, Jackie, and I built a log cabin in the Idaho wilderness. Our two nearest neighbors were seven and thirty seven miles from us. The Sawtooths are abundant in animals; elk, deer, moose, mountain lions, bears, bobcats, goats, the elusive wolf, and the ferocious wolverine. We were neighbors to these animals and many more.

When we moved into the wilderness, I had hunted for over thirty years and thought I knew something about the habits of the animals. During the first few months at our new home I realized how much I could learn from our wonderful environment. For seven years, I chose not to kill. The experience I gained during that time was remarkable.

It was my habit to feed Quest, our three legged German Shepherd, each evening at twilight. I would also toss a handful of dry dog food into the feeder for the Stellar jays, just to help tide them over the days of ever deepening snow and plunging temperatures. One night I had just fed Quest when he started barking. I looked out the window and in the dim light I could see him cautiously approaching the feeder. At the feeder was a large fox, holding her ground. Quest gained confidence and moved closer. The fox hesitated, then broke and ran. The dog took up the chase, barking furiously. Shortly, he came back up the trail with his tongue hanging out.

The following night, I fed Quest inside and put part of a can of dog food in the feeder. Quest ate and curled up in front of the fireplace, a treat for him. I was in my study when he sensed the intruder and began barking. I went to the window and there was the fox. She was quickly taking the dog food. In an instant, the food was gone and so was the fox.

For days, the temperature had plunged below freezing. At night, I could hear the rifle shot retort of trees popping as the bark froze. For several of these harsh winter days, I continued to feed the fox. Quest still went crazy when she appeared, but he enjoyed his time inside.

The fox grew more confident each night, as she came for her meal. In time, she was not disturbed when I remained outside on the porch, a short distance of only twenty feet from where she fed. With each feeding, she ate more slowly and did not bolt, but rather trotted back down the trail. As she let down her defense, I began to question my actions in feeding her. There is an old saying that you can make wild ducks tame but you can't make tame ducks wild. If the fox grew dependent on me, how would she fend for herself? I wondered if I was helping her or perhaps, in the long run, harming her. I decided to stop the feeding and let her return to a normal existence.

The first night after I decided to stop feeding her, I took Quest's food out to him. I did not fill the feeder. I waited and watched from inside the cabin. The fox trotted up the trail and Quest started barking. He immediately bound down the trail after her. Upon realizing that Quest was loose and coming after her, she stopped, spun around and dashed down the hill. The quarter mile path, a result of weeks of cross country skiing, was an exhilarating glide winding from our cabin down a small hill and into a large meadow. The Snow was a hard pack with a topping of light snow. Exhausted, Quest finally returned. This game of fox and hound continued for several nights and I tried to observe each chase.

The next night, Quest responded as usual and started his pursuit down the trail. The sound of his barking weakened as he headed for the meadow. I waited and watched and, to my surprise, the fox came running up to the porch and dashed to the dog dish. I could hear the dog barking in the distance while the fox hurriedly helped herself to his dinner and ran away. Quest returned, even more tired than from previous chases, unaware that his evening meal was missing.

I watched this routine for several more nights, wondering how the fox was beating Quest back to the house. One bright full moonlit evening, I back tracked her and was amused at what I unraveled. The tracks revealed that each night the fox changed her approach to the cabin. She would provoke Quest into the chase then, far down in the meadow, jump from the hard frozen ski trail onto the soft powdered snow and run lightly back up to the cabin, always from a fresh approach. Quest would follow only to become bogged down by his weight, forcing him to break new trail each night. The fox had ample time to take his food before Quest could return. One night, the game changed. The technique worked until Quest got smarter and returned on the ski trail, forcing her to give up her ploy. She soon moved on. I now have a better understanding of the statement,

"Smart like a fox."

I had the opportunity to experience so many wonderful animals. Eagles and ravens were my friends. I was able to approach an old six point bull elk to within three feet. I spent time with the wolf and mountain lion. The lessons I learned were far greater than those gained in thirty years of hunting.

Spend as much time as you can in the environment in which you choose to hunt. Learn the terrain. *Be silent and observe*. Study the animals' habits. This is all invaluable basic knowledge to a hunter. The *three secrets* of good hunters are that *they truly know the animals they hunt*, and therefore they can anticipate the animals actions. Second, *they know the terrain and habitat in which they hunt*, and can use it to their advantage. Last, but most important, *they keep hunting with patience, persistence and strong perseverance.*

"smart like a fox"

I will become expert with the weapon I choose so that my aim will be true.

The first time you must finish the life of a wounded animal, you will appreciate a clean kill. *A hunter must know his weapon and be expert with it*. A hunter who goes into the field unprepared to make a sure hit can count on a bad experience. I have watched a poor shot knock all the legs out from under a muley buck, yet take three more shots to stop it and put it out of pain. The suffering brought to an animal through unskillful marksmanship is a high price for not mastering your weapon.

I will make my kill as humane as possible and render the coup de grace immediately, if necessary, to insure the least suffering.

"Coup de grace" is a french term meaning "stroke of mercy." It is the death blow or a shot administered to end the suffering of a mortally wounded animal.

My Grandfather started me fishing at a very young age. He gave me an important lesson when I was only four or five years old. He had helped me rig a fishing pole and showed me a spot to fish. In an instant I had a small rainbow trout on the line. I reeled it in, took the hook out and dropped it on the bank. The sparkling fish flipped and twisted on the earth. I started to bait up when my Grandfather approached, picked up the fish, placed his thumb in it's mouth, then quickly snapped the head back, breaking the spine. He told me that he had made a deal a long time ago, he promised the trout that he would not let them suffer when he caught them. He felt it was a special agreement which made him a friend of the fish. In his thinking, the fish communicated to the other fish that he was a fair and good fisherman. He would take more care in releasing a trout than anyone I have known. He also caught more fish than most people.

My Grandfather would never let any animal suffer. A quickly cut throat or shot to the base of the head is a sure way to end the animal's life.

If you cut the throat, make the cut low and at the front base of the neck directly above the bone structure of the sternum. Cut deep and across, so as to severe the windpipe and jugular. Take special care in your cut if you desire to save the animal's cape. A shot to the head should be placed at the base of the ear and towards the brain stem. A shot so placed will immediately end the animals life with the least suffering.

As a hunter, you must be able to administer the "coup de grace." Do it quickly with confidence and respect for the animal.

"their eyes...they seek
they are the watchers"

I know that the taking of an animal's life is a profound lesson. I pledge to

understand and respect this experience as a key element in learning the meaning of life. I will waste no part of an animal. To waste a gift of nature is intolerable to me. Because of this, I will make every effort to track and finish any wounded animal.

I cannot tolerate hunters who willfully waste game. I remember one fall in Utah when the Fish and Game department changed the regulation on the bag limit on redhead ducks because of a startling report on the diminishing numbers of this species. The Fish and Game received the data just weeks prior to the opening of the general duck season. They reacted by making a last minute change intended to dramatically reduced the harvest of redheads. The change came so late that many hunters did not have the time to learn the skills needed to distinguish redheads from other ducks, especially the hens in flight. That same fall I was hunting at Farmington Bay, Utah with a group of good friends. The area was popular due to its close proximity to Salt Lake City and Ogden, coupled with a wonderful waterfowl population and habitat. On that opening morning there were well over one thousand hunters positioned around the widespread marshes and waterways. The season opened at 12:00 pm. The first shot rang out, a second, a third, and then the firing erupted into the thunderous sound of an infantry battle. Ducks blackened the sky in flight. In every direction I turned, there were flocks of redheads. Birds were falling out of the sky like bombers going through intense flack.

The shooting continued steadily for about fifteen minutes then slowed to one or two shots from random blinds. Almost every duck that had come over me was a redhead with the exception of a few mallards, canvas back and teal. Hunters started leaving the marsh in late afternoon, laden with birds. As hunters compared their kill with each other, they learned that most of the ducks they had in their possession were redheads. The information quickly went through the marsh. Many hunters had been unable to properly identify a redhead, while others were simply unaware of the late regulation change.

Throughout the marsh, you could hear the sucking sound of boots stomping redheads into the mud. Walking the trails back, I could see the holes with fresh feathers poking from the black bog. Redheads were hidden in the cattails and thrown in the water. There is no doubt thousands of redheads were wasted that day. This was a painful and profound lesson for many of the hunters. It is imperative that you know the correct identification of the animals you hunt. Last year we found the wasted remains of three moose that were either willfully killed, with the full knowledge they were illegal, or less likely that the hunters did not have the skill to know the difference between an elk and a moose. In either case, there was no excuse for wasting the life of these majestic animals.

The last elk I killed was during the last light of the final day of the season. I was hunting with a friend, Dick Steel. Dick had been raised near the area in which we were hunting and had hunted and trapped there for most of his life. The shot was a long one of about three hundred and fifty yards. The elk, a big bull, dropped where he stood. There was fresh snow on the ground and it was quickly getting dark.

To get to the elk, we had to cross a deep canyon filled with windfall. We watched the elk, giving it time to die. It is important to give an animal sufficient time to finish its life. If you move too quickly the animal will draw on deep strength to get away, forcing you to spend time and energy in tracking. We waited for about ten or fifteen minutes. I could barely see the elk in the dim light, but it had not moved. I started towards it and Dick stayed on the ridge to help me spot the elk. Crossing the canyon was difficult. I was frequently tangled and blocked by fallen trees and heavy brush. I climbed out of the canyon and could vaguely make out Dick on the other side. With the help of Dick's directions, I worked my way up to where the elk was hit.

I spotted the tree by which I had marked the elk then located the area in which he had fallen. There was no elk, only a patch of bright red blood where he had fallen. Dick was already on his way into the canyon. Daylight was almost gone. I scouted the elk's trail for several hundred feet.

The tracks were clear in the snow with small puddles of blood every fifty feet or so.

I returned to meet Dick. Judging from the bright red color of the blood as well as the amount he was losing, my feeling was that he was hit hard in the lungs and would soon go down. We were miles away from our camp. We talked. Dick agreed that the sign looked as though the elk couldn't move far. We decided to track him although it was nearly dark. Good trackers have a sixth sense that allows them to follow a track even in dim light and Dick had that special gift.

We walked the track, moving downhill for about fifteen minutes. The track was clear and the bleeding had continued, but droppings were less frequent. We spotted where he had laid down. The snow was flattened and blood stained but not as much nor as bright as where he had first fallen. A clear track went downhill from his resting place. We trailed the elk, finding seven more resting spots marked with blood. We had moved down the mountain to a point where the snow was almost gone making it much more difficult to continue tracking. We spent the night curled up around a pinion fire with heated rocks tucked around us to keep warm. The trick of using heated rocks has saved me from many cold sub-zero temperature nights. This technique is a handy tool to understand.

At first light, we found the trail again. The ground was now loose slate, bare of snow. The bleeding had stopped except for an occasional drop or smear. We followed the trail until almost dark and were led to a large, open sagebrush knoll. The ground was hard and mostly rock. Mixed with many other tracks in a maze of game trails, we lost the elk's tracks.

The last rays of the sun were piercing the twilight as it dropped behind a distant mountain. We talked. We were far from camp but near a well traveled road. We were about to give up and head for the road when I saw a glimpse of sunray reflect from something on the sage flat below us. I told Dick that I wanted to check it out. I had a strange hunch that it was the elk. I marked the spot where I had seen the reflection by the location of a large sage. Marking, or spotting, is a must technique for locating downed animals. Look for a prominent land feature as a marker. Locate your kill in respect to the marker. You may need to use sub-markers for further location. An example would be a bright grove of Quaken Aspen, at the bottom of a unique rock outcropping. The sun was now down and darkness was descending fast. I walked to the sage and then to where I thought I had seen the reflection. There was nothing there. I looked in every direction. No elk.

My hunch was still quite strong. The last light was giving way to nightfall as I started walking in a growing circle outward around the sage. The light was finally gone. About one hundred feet from the sage, I stumbled in the darkness. There under my feet were the antlers of the elk protruding from a large patch of sagebrush where he had fallen dead. We field dressed the elk, marked the spot with a red handkerchief and headed for the road.

The elk, a large six point, had been hit in the chest. The shot had entered at an angle and had barely clipped one lung. The animal had traveled over twenty rough miles and for more than twenty hours in that condition. Consider the power and will to live that the elk possessed. How many men could do the same? A good and responsible hunter must have the respect, strength, and will to keep tracking. Never give up. I know of many fine guides and hunters who tell stories of even longer tracking efforts in order to avoid wasting an animal.

The spirit to hunt is natural, but the attitude to waste is not. My Grandfather had some thoughts on taking an animal. As with fish, he had made a pact with the animals. He would not waste them. In respect, they would be there for his needs. He was one of the best and most successful hunters I have known. I accepted his lesson and have never gone hungry, even when living from the land for extended periods of time. Have respect for the animal you hunt. Don't waste any part of it. If you cant use the meat, hide or any other part of the animal, give it to someone who needs the food or can use the materials. This attitude will assist you in being a better and more responsible hunter.

"the osprey uses his weapon wisely,
strikes quickly and sure,
eats what he kills"

I am an honest hunter and obey all hunting laws. I support the officers who enforce these laws.

The men and women who make up Fish and Game Departments are dedicated individuals working for the benefit of wildlife, conservation, and hunters. Not surprisingly, most of them work in this field because of their love for nature and the animals which it supports and protects.

Regretfully, some of these good people have given their lives in the enforcement of conservation laws. They need and deserve the help and support of all good hunters. The task they perform has helped us conserve and build animal populations and habitats at a time when others have forgotten the need for wildlife on this planet. Through good control and management, I have witnessed animal populations return to areas where they had nearly been wiped out by the forces of modern civilization.

Several years ago, I was hunting in an area called Cherry Creek, a place well known for massive mule deer bucks. The herd was experiencing heavy winter kill due to increased farming and land clearing. Acres of Buck Brush, Pinion and Juniper forests were being ripped from the ground with large chains pulled between D8 cats.

The effect of the clearing was evident everywhere. The cedar breaks were littered with the bones of deer that had died in the preceding severe winter. I found the remains of over fifty deer in one canyon. Because of the shrinking habitat, the Game Department had opened a special hunt with multiple tags for either sex in the area. I had hunted a long cedar ridge, pushing a small doe and late fawn down before me. The fawn had barely lost its spots. They stopped near a clump of juniper on the sidehill about one hundred feet below me.

I squatted in the warm sun next to a rugged old juniper to relax and watch them. A truck came up a dirt road about two hundred feet below the deer, and stopped. The men in the truck, two up front and three in the back, jumped out and pointed at the doe and fawn. In an instant they all had rifles aimed and firing at the deer. The first rounds hit the ground between the doe and fawn. The frightened doe made one fast bound uphill into the juniper cover and disappeared. The fawn was frozen in place, not seeing the doe, it did not know how to react. Shots were slapping the ground around it. After many shots, it was finally hit in a rear leg. It got up and was hit again in the stomach. It tried to get up one more time when it was finally killed by a shot to it's spine.

The men had not seen me. One of them climbed up to the fawn, grabbed it by the hind legs and held up its light body with one arm. It could not have weighed over forty-five pounds. The man swung it back and forth as he hollered down to the others that it was too small and shot to hell like hamburger. My anger grew as he shouted and swung the fawn. With his last swing, he released the fawn, it flew in an arc, landing in the junipers.

I was enraged. I stood up, shouted "HOLD IT", and started toward him with my rifle at ready arms. He had a pained, startled look on his face as I approached. I said just three words, "Tag it now" He looked at me for a long moment, then at his friends below. I did not say another word. I just stood there and watched him clean, tag and carry out less than forty pounds of shot up meat. I also hoped he carried some shame and guilt with him.

A good hunter must know the law and respect it. Outlaws and renegade hunters hurt the animals as well as the efforts of good hunters. Don't hesitate to help an officer when needed. *We must all work together in the process of conservation and wildlife management.*

"only through man's stupidity
do we show bad ethics"

"new life...promise
a renewing of spirit"

CONCEPTS FOR SURVIVAL

Written by
Garn G. Christensen

A book that can save your life in more than one way; in the wilderness or in your everyday survival.

The concepts I will give you were developed from living in the wilderness. They are basic to wilderness survival however, I hope you will find them universal in their application and useful in daily life.

A woman stopped me on the street and asked for help. She was neat and clean and I judged her age to be over sixty. It was my feeling she was not a "professional panhandler". She told me she was stranded in our city. No money, no one to turn to. I gave her the change from my pockets and we talked for a few minutes. "This" had never happened to her before; there had always been work and a home. This winter, the streets were home and, day by day, she survived on faith and the good will of others.

Your need may be the first time you find yourself lost while hunting or alone in a strange wilderness. Or, as the woman, alienated from the familiar security of the past and confronting an unknown future. The application of these principles can get you through some rough times.

In Fall of 1978, I was selected as a member of a special three man team contracted by the U.S. Army to instruct helicopter pilots on survival skills. I had been chosen because of the survival training I had done with commercial and private pilots. I had also taught survival skills while serving in the Army.

The Army wanted the school to be basic in concept as it would serve as a universal foundation for survival and confidence skills needed in a variety of environments and conditions. The immediate environment of concern for these pilots was the Mideast.

My companions on the team were Dr. Robert "PK" Keller and Larry Dean Olsen. Bob is one of the nation's leading experts on emergency trauma medicine and a pioneer in wilderness medicine. Larry is a specialist on the physical aspects of survival: fire, water, food and shelter. Most of his vast knowledge is based on his study of primitive North Americans, especially the Anasazi tribe. He may well have trained more individuals on survival skill development than any other person in the United States. His book, *Outdoor Survival Skills,* is a classic and is required reading by anyone seriously seeking an understanding of wilderness living.

It was my responsibility to give instruction on psychological and philosophical concepts for survival. My expertise developed from experience and detailed analysis of many difficult survival circumstances. I have also gained knowledge from studying with Indian friends. Everything I have taught was personally field tested under a wide variety of conditions and resources.

My knowledge of survival has strong personal roots and I was not sure how the pilots would react to a program that asked them to abandon the high technology to which they had grown attached and rely upon their individual inner strengths.

The site chose for the survival training was a remote area known as "The Indians" located within the protection of the Hunter Legit Military Base near King City, California. The Indians had been turned over to the U.S. Forest Service by the estate of William Randolph Hearst. Prior to white settlement, it had been home to a tribe of coastal Indians.

The area had been protected with such care that it was common to find old campsites stocked with ancient tools and implements. The terrain there was unique in two ways. First, it had a greater variety of plants in one single small area than in any other part of North America. This is due to the rapid change in habitat as you climb quickly from the California Big Sur Coast up to the arid Marble Mountains. It is an ideal location to teach abroad spectrum of survival skills and techniques, especially when you are working with a large number of helicopters. The second unique feature of The Indians is the high incidence of poison ivy and poison oak. In some locations as much as seventy-five percent of the underbrush is hostile. It was interesting to note that historical reports indicate that the plants had no effect on the Indians. This seems to be confirmed by the fact that I found old arrow shafts made from poison ivy wood. Since it contained all the elements and materials required for survival, the location was ideal for a tough but relatively kind survival environment.

The students were stripped of technology to only a knife and blanket and challenged to gain control of their reality by using the Earth around them. The truth, they learned, was not to challenge life or the Earth but, rather, to work with it. Those who were willing to understand and work with the environment found that the Earth is an abundant provider.

I will use the same format in giving you basic survival information as I did when I presented it to the pilots.

When you find yourself in a survival situation, it will be too late to make preparations. You must use what you have at hand to survive. The first and most important rule for survival is an old one and was well understood by a man of wisdom, Sir Robert Baden Powell, founder of the Boy Scouts. He adopted the rule, **BE PREPARED**, as a motto for the organization. There is no substitute for preparation.

One preparation rule you must always observe is to have the proper clothing and footwear for the worst conditions you might expect to encounter. I have seen inexperienced pilots fly across vast wilderness areas, which were subject to violent weather changes, clothed only in a t-shirt, shorts, thongs, and without any survival gear. These individuals are looking for trouble.

In almost every survival experience in which there were fatalities, there was no preparation in training nor in the availability of basic survival materials and tools. I strongly recommend that any person who hunts or desires to live or work in the wilderness have a basic survival kit. It can make the difference between life and death. These supplies can be very simple with little weight and cost, or you may wish to include more items which can increase your opportunity for survival.

A survival kit developed in New Zealand is so small that all the items it contains can be stored in the tube of a pen size flashlight with the batteries removed. This minikit contains matches (waterproofed in a drinking straw filled with paraffin wax), water purification tablets, a magnetized needle used suspended from a silk thread as a compass or for suturing wounds, safety pin for securing bandages, an injector type razor blade used as a knife, a birthday candle for light and fire starter, a small roll of fine wire, and sheet of aluminum foil to be used in a variety of ways (cooking utensil, water container, signaling device).

The contents of your survival kit will depend on the type of country and terrain in which you plan to operate. The following items are basic to almost all survival situations and a wise person going into the wilderness will make sure they are available in case of emergency.

1.   A good sharp knife with a carbon steel blade. If necessary, it can be used as a striking steel in creating fire with flint or other spark

producing rocks.

2.   Materials to create a fire. Carry a lighter, waterproofed matches, tinder, candles, and water proofed fire starting devices.

3.   A good lightweight canteen or other water container, filled and emptied before and after each expedition. The advantage of a metal container is that it can be used to boil water.

4.   A working flashlight, with extra batteries, for light and signaling.

5.   Emergency medical kit.

6.   Water purification tablets and five feet of rubber surgical tubing 1/4 inch in diameter.

7.   Two lightweight emergency blankets. Foil space blankets work well, are lightweight and will serve a number of needs.

8.   A supply of high energy, lightweight food.

9.   Signal devices such as a small pilots signaling mirror and a loud police whistle.

10.   Compass and area map.

11.   A twelve foot by twelve foot sheet of plastic. It is light in weight and serves for shelter and water accumulation.

12.   Thirty feet of nylon parachute or rip cord.

An important point to remember is that <u>you can survive with only the items you find in nature,</u> but the more you think out what you will require the better prepared you will be to survive, an emergency, should it occur.

A prudent individual will make sure they have a sound working knowledge of emergency medical procedures. This training can be as fundamental as a basic Red Cross First Aid Course or as advanced as E.M.T. (Emergency Medical Technician) training. This training should be repeated often enough so that your information and skills are current. A periodic review of emergency medical procedures may save your life or the life of a friend. Make it a priority to take first aid training before going into the field.

The last, but most important, consideration in being prepared is your attitude. A positive attitude can save your life. After studying case histories and experiencing survival techniques under a variety of harsh environmental field conditions, I have extracted a philosophy that has proven to be essential in sustaining life even under conditions that seem to be beyond survival.

The beginning point of this survival philosophy is a strong commitment to life. In 1987, the Wall Street Journal published what I feel is a good definition of the meaning of commitment. I found peace in these words and will share them with you:

> Commitment is what transforms a promise into reality. It is the words that speak boldly of your intentions and the actions which speak louder than words. It is making time when there is none...coming through time after time, year after year. Commitment is the stuff character is made of...the power to change the face of things. It is the daily triumph of integrity over skepticism.
>
> *-author unknown*

Without commitment, there is little chance to make it through a difficult situation. No matter how hard survival becomes, never give up. Keep your will to live. You will make it.

I have spent much time working with severely injured and handicapped individuals. They have been some of my best teachers. The most memorable was Juan, a young migrant farm worker, who had lost his primary arm at the shoulder in a farming accident. The accident had occurred two years prior to our trip into the wilderness. He had been fitted with an artificial limb but never used it and had become completely dependent upon the care given by others. He was discouraged and, feeling he had no further reason to live, Juan had not responded to normal rehabilitation treatment techniques. Filled with self-pity and frustration, Juan had given up. He felt he could only survive with the help of others. As a last resort, I was asked to work with him.

My approach was a survival course in the wilderness with limited supplies. I wanted to start with the basics. Juan spoke very little English; I spoke very little Spanish. My assistant, Bill Chisholm, was a bit more proficient in Spanish than I, but not much.

We set up camp the first day of training. I will never forget the look on Juan's face when I communicated to him that it was his job to gather firewood and get the fire going. I told him we needed the fire to cook and keep warm, and without it we would not have a meal. Further, it would be a very cold night! Reluctantly, he began gathering wood, one stick at a time. Bill and I continued setting up camp and ignored Juan. Soon he was bringing in arms full of wood, using the artificial limb as a brace to hold the collected wood in his good arm. Piece by piece, he brought in a large store of wood. His attitude changed as he saw the pile grow. He had a smile on his face when he finally kindled his first fire. When his fire burst into full flame, so did his will to live. He had taken the first step in gaining control of his life.

The next ten days were hard. There were times when Juan wanted to give up and grew angry with the tasks assigned to him. In the end, he was able to use his new arm and could do almost anything we could. He used basic tools, knife, hammer, shovel, saw, and ax. As his successes grew, so did his positive attitude.

When we finished the training, Juan had the confidence that he could make it in life without the help to which he had become so addicted. The most important lesson for him was the need for commitment to life. Once he had regained that commitment, self confidence and a positive mental attitude soon followed.

Through my experience, I have found some fundamental principles that have helped individuals survive critical situations. These concepts are common factors in all of the successful survival cases I have studied as well as those I have lived through.

The first thing that must be done when planning a trip is to tell a responsible person of your plans, including where you are going, a detailed map of your route, where you expect to camp, and any other information concerning your movement during the trip. Inform the person or persons of your departure and return date. Pilots call this a Flight Plan. This information is critical if a search and rescue operation is necessary.

The time it saves can mean the difference between life and death.

The first rule for survival is simple; **CONSERVE ENERGY**. Once you find yourself in a survival situation, **DON'T PANIC. PANIC IS A KILLER** and wastes vital energy. The moment you realize you are in trouble stop, sit down and get comfortable and think about getting control of yourself. Place both hands on the ground. In fact, dig your fingers into the earth. This contact has a beneficial and quieting effect. Next, start breathing in a slow, deep, deliberate manner, taking about fifteen to twenty breaths per minute. Continue for two or three minutes or until you feel relaxed.

I call this grounding. It will prevent the harmful physical effects of panic and fear. As you breathe, take time to assess your situation. Inventory the tools and supplies you have. Above all, don't allow panic to control your actions. Most uninjured persons who die in survival circumstances are the victims of panic. Some have been known to run away from their supplies and gear because they were overcome by panic. Out of control and exhausted from wasted effort, they die from exposure.

Your physical strength and mental ability will be at its height right at the moment you realize you're in trouble. In fact, it may be higher than normal as a result of the effects of adrenaline. Your energy level will be high for several hours. As the adrenaline wears off, you may experience a real let down. Now is the time you must conserve energy and get your survival plan into operation. Individuals who do not make it through a survival problem have three factors in common: 1) they give up the will to live, 2) they forget the basics, and 3) they panic. To avoid these traps, keep your mind focused on a successful survival, not on the fear of being lost or dying.

Once you have gained control, your next action is of great importance. If you are injured or lost, you must decide whether to stay where you are or attempt to find your way back to familiar country. My advice, as well as the advice of experts, is to stay near the location where you first realize you are in trouble. This is especially true if you have informed someone of your plans.

I know of a pilot who was forced down in a remote mountain area and escaped the crash uninjured. He crashed in an area of abundant survival supplies such as wood, shelter, water, and food. His aircraft was also a storehouse of survival materials. Even though he was overweight and not in condition to push his physical endurance, he left a note in the plane that he had seen lights in the distance and was going to walk out. The note was vague, giving neither the time he left nor the direction he intended to travel. He had filed a flight plan and the aircraft was located within twenty four hours, but the search and rescue party spent the next seven days looking for him. His body was found in a deep wooded canyon only a few miles from the crash site. He had died from exhaustion and exposure. Wilderness and desert terrain can be cruelly deceptive. What appears to be very near can be, in actuality, much further, especially if you must cross rough deep canyons or arid country. This problem ties into a basic survival concept; **ADMIT YOU'RE LOST**.

All too often a person will not admit he or she is lost or has a severe problem. They lie to themselves and engage in aimless, energy wasting activity that severely hinders their chances for survival. I have helped locate individuals who wandered in circles for days, out of control and near death.

Once you acknowledge you have a problem, you can take corrective action. Otherwise, you are wasting precious time and energy. The concept of **HONESTY** has a strong bearing on all aspects of your life. You will be amazed at how many problems are solved with this one concept.

If you have informed someone of your schedule (your flight plan) they can get help to you quickly. Setup your camp, have signals ready, conserve energy, and be patient. Remember, most rescues occur within seventy-two hours, but with a positive mental attitude, you can survive for a much longer period of time if necessary.

The next concept for survival is that you must assume **PERSONAL RESPONSIBILITY FOR YOUR SURVIVAL**. No one but you can be responsible for your life. Many people neglect to learn the basic skills needed to provide shelter and fire or find food and water because they assume they will be rescued should they become lost. You must live your own life and take responsibility for your realities. True security comes from discovering inner strength.

Once panic is under control, you must get your survival program started immediately. Preparations should be made to live under survival conditions for a prolonged period of time. Conserve energy and make every expenditure of energy count. If you take a walk to set signals, don't return to camp empty handed; look for wood or other materials you may need. Let your expended energy serve two or three needs rather than just one.

My daughter's Godfather, Thomas Beanka, is one of the Elders of the Hopi tribe. He gave me some good advice when he told me, "everything you need at any given moment is within thirty feet of you. You will be amazed by what is right at hand. But you must always remember you are the center of the circle; the best survival tool you have is your own mind. Think. Use your mind for creative adaptation."

As advised, stay near the location where you first realize you are in trouble. This does not mean you must stay rooted to the spot but should pick the nearest and best location that will give you the greatest chance to survive. Choose a location with good visibility where you or your signals can be spotted by air or ground search. Select a site with the best opportunity for shelter, fuel, water, and food. The right site selection is an important factor to help you conserve energy.

One of your first priorities will be fire. There is some ancient need to have the comfort and security of a fire. I recommend that you start a fire promptly, even if it is summer. The fire not only makes you feel better but also serves as a signaling device. Many hunters and pilots have tried to get a signal fire started when they heard the engine of an approaching search plane, only to get the fire going at a useful level after the plane had flown over.

One of the most difficult aspects of survival is sitting and waiting without something to keep you occupied. Tending a fire keeps your mind off the fact that you are alone and gives you something to do. The fire will soon become your friend and be ready as a signal when needed. Merlin, the magician of King Arthur's Court said the first magic given to men and the last to be taken away is fire.

One of the most common mistakes in fire making is not having all the necessary materials together before attempting to start the fire. Hopefully, you will be prepared and have fire making supplies in your survival kit.

Carry items that give you the greatest possibility in starting a fire, even under severe and adverse conditions. The principles of fire construction is one of graduation of combustible materials starting with tinder, fire-starter, and then very small slivers of kindling, larger sticks of kindling and then bigger sticks of wood. Have all the materials gathered before you start. This will give you the best opportunity for a good fire.

The easiest fire structure is a simple pyramid or tepee structure. Place your tinder on a foundation of dry sticks laid as a base. Then place the kindling and larger material in a cone pattern around the fire starter and tinder. Start with small sticks then progressively add larger sticks. Keep space between the material to allow for the air to feed the fire. If you have a chemical starter or can find pitch from conifers, pine, spruce, or other evergreen trees, add this to your tinder and small kindling. This will give you a good start even under difficult conditions.

Fire loves to climb. Place one long stick of wood vertically in the center of your fire cone. Let it extend a foot or more above the cone. It will act like a magnet, drawing the fire up through the cone.

You may need a fire when conditions are wet. Dry fire material can usually be found even in very wet weather if you know where to look. The best place to find tinder and dry wood is at the base of older trees or under windfall. This is especially true of most conifers. Look under rock overhangs or other natural shelters. I have found excellent tinder in old animal dens. Sift the dirt at the entrance and in the bottom of the den with your open fingers. It is surprising how much bone dry tinder is often hidden in the debris.

Even if you cannot find dry tinder, there is always a way. One rainy fall, I was in Kentucky teaching a survival course in conjunction with a university group. The course was primarily on how to mentally approach a survival situation. The major lesson was that no matter where you are or what the conditions may be, you have at hand the means to survive. The key to this lesson was that you could create fire from the elements and materials nature provides; fire from just the Earth's resources without matches, lighter, or commercial fire starters. It had rained for several days and the hardwood forests were soaked. No matter how hard I searched, I could not find dry tinder to use with the bow drill which I had created from native materials. We were working in a down pour and everything was sopping wet. Dry tinder would not yield to my search. I was not sure I would be able to demonstrate fire from nature. I stopped my efforts and reviewed the basics. I looked at the thirty foot circle around me. I knew I had the answer within myself if I would use my best tool- my mind. Dry the tinder

I took the wet tinder and put it inside my clothing next to my skin under my arm pits and in my groin. Hopefully, heat from these warm body centers would dry the tinder. Next, I observed another survival rule: **PATIENCE, PERSISTENCE and PERSEVERANCE**. I patiently split the wet sticks in pieces, breaking them apart to get to the dryer inner layers. I persevered in finishing the bow drill to its most efficient level. I persisted in believing the fire would start. After several hours of work and preparation, I brought out the tinder. I had separated it to give the greatest exposure to body heat. Each small handful was nearly dry and I gently blew on it to complete the process. It was late in the afternoon and the rain continued. With one small bundle of semi-dry tinder, I started methodically working the bow drill. At last the friction produced by the drill gave me a small smoking pile of dark brown wood dust with a tiny crimson ember glowing at its center.

I gently dropped the ember into the tinder bundle and started blowing lightly. A wisp of smoke grew in the bundle as the heart of the ember increased ever so slowly in brightness. Finally, it burst into flames. I slipped the burning tinder into the fire cone I had prepared. The fire hesitated and started to die. I dropped to my knees and started to softly blow. I had no more tinder. As I blew, the sparks recovered. For almost fifteen minutes, I continued my effort with the fire vacillating between life and death. Just as I thought the fire would go out, I made another effort. Soon everyone was helping to sustain the steady air supply. It was only our belief in ourselves that kept us trying. The kindling burst into flame and quickly the fire was burning strong.

Start every fire as though your life depended upon it and that you are using your last dry tinder or your only match. Make careful preparation and never give up until you succeed. I was truly amazed to get fire that wet stormy day. It certainly helped reinforce the lesson.

When you are lost or need help, fire is your best friend. Keep the fire burning and use good management. Obtain and maintain a supply of dry wood. A small fire will keep you warm, serve other needs, and conserve your fuel supply.

Smoke from a fire is an excellent signal. There is also surveillance of many areas for fire control. These observers may spot your fire. To increase smoke, keep green foliage nearby such as pine boughs or fresh grass. The smoke can be seen by aircraft or from a distant search and rescue observer.

Spend the time to understand fire creation. It is one of the best skills you can learn. If ever you must make it through a sub-zero winter night, alone in the wilderness after falling in a river, you will understand the need for fire.

Your next priority will be water. Normally, you can function without water for seventy-two hours. Should you find yourself in a survival situation, hopefully you will have had the foresight to have a water container with you. This water will serve your immediate need but you must begin looking for other sources right away.

Ground water is common in most terrains. Water will always be at the lowest ground feature. Water gives life to vegetation so look for your water source in vegetated canyon bottoms or other depressions in the earth. Plant growth is a good indicator of where water may be located. I have often found water in arid locations, in potholes or depressions in the rocks.

Another source of water is the dew that forms on plants and objects at night. You must use your head and the resources available. A pilot ran out of fuel over a remote location in the Baja desert and was forced to land. The plane was not damaged and neither was he injured. He had not filed a flight plan nor did he carry survival gear or water. After many days, the pilot died of dehydration. Rescuers finally located the plane one morning and noted that the wings were covered with dew. Had he known it, the pilot could have collected enough water each day to save his life. The water was on the wings of his aircraft right over his head each morning but he did not have the knowledge, observation skills or common sense to realize it was there. Remember this lesson and check the leaves of vegetation in the morning for collected dew.

Most water found in natural conditions will need to be purified. The safest purification process is to boil any water before drinking. The rule to purify water is to boil it for five minutes plus one additional minute for each one thousand feet of elevation. There are some water contaminates that can only be eliminated by boiling. If you have purification tablets or a tested filter, use them.

If you have the items I suggested for your survival kit, you will be able to make a solar water still. The earth contains moisture and will give it to you through evaporation. To make the still, dig a hole three feet deep and four feet wide. You can make a digging stick from a small tree or limb. Cut the plastic into a six foot by six foot square. Place an open container in the center and at the bottom of your pit. Curl the surgical tube in the bottom of the collector, then run the tube to the outside of the pit so it may be used as a drinking straw. Let it come out of the pit and lay it to the side of the hole. Place the 6' by 6' piece of plastic over the top of the hole. Place a small rock on the center of the plastic So it will form an inverted cone with the bottom of the cone directly over the water collector but don't allow the plastic to touch the collector. Cover the outer edge of the plastic with dirt in order to give the still a closed airtight seal. Water evaporating from the earth will accumulate on the underside of the plastic surface and drip into the collector.

You can then sip the collected water from the collector directly through the surgical tubing without disturbing the still. You can increase your water production by filling the bottom of the still with crushed vegetation. There have been cases when individuals have been in such need of water that they drank urine, blood or other liquids such as coolants from a radiator. All can kill you. Urine or other questionable sources of water can be placed in a second open container in the Solar still, separate and away from your collector. The water collected will be drinkable due to the distillation process. The solar still can give you pure water each day.

This is a survival skill you must master prior to needing it in an emergency. It is much easier to carry the required materials, otherwise you will have to use creative adaptations of materials at hand. The surgical tubing can also serve other purposes such as a sling shot, finger flipper, for hunting small rodents, reptiles, birds, or bungee cord.

In mountain locations, a common water problem is giardia or "beaver fever". This is a parasitical cyst that can only be destroyed by boiling or using a special filter device. There is a drinking straw filter on the market that is lightweight and effective.

The last but most important thought on water is to use your head. Be prepared. You can live a long time without food but water is a must so put it high on your priority list. There are also some tricks in conserving water. Limit your activities. If you must move about or work, do it at night. Don't eat, or eat smaller quantities, as digestion requires water. Leave your clothes on to reduce evaporation from your skin. If you have ample water, use it. The best canteen you may have with you is your stomach. If it comes down to a choice of drinking water that may be biologically contaminated or dying from dehydration, drink the water. Medical technology can kill the bugs but cannot bring back your life.

Food is not as important as you might think. You can function for a long time without food. I have often lived off the land for weeks. This subject requires much more attention than I can give you in this basic information.

If you are prepared, you will have emergency food with you. If you don't, remember, **THE FIRST RULE OF SURVIVAL IS CONSERVATION OF ENERGY.** Therefore, the best source of food will require the least effort to obtain.

I had given this rule to a class for private and executive pilots. Despite having been given the rule, they proceeded to waste most of a day chasing a covey of pine grouse (fool chickens) up and down mountains and rough canyons. They never got the grouse but of much more significance was the amount of energy wasted in their effort.

In a survival situation, I use two primary sources of food. The first source is the edible plants around me. You can quickly gain a knowledge of basic edible plants by studying the reference books already mentioned or, better yet, by working with an experienced herbalist. Always make sure you are certain of proper plant identification. If you have the slightest doubt about a plant, don't eat it. There are about 20 plants common to many locations that make up my menu. If I am not sure of a plant, I leave it alone. An inexperienced river guide served deadly water hemlock to his guest thinking it was wild parsnip. It killed him.

A good standby is grass. It is one of the most common and plentiful plants on earth. The grass may be chewed for its moisture and sugar content. Don't swallow the bulk or fiber, only the juice. The fiber can cause stomach problems. The stem of grass can be eaten and is sweet with fructose. Most kids have chewed the end of a grass stem and know what I'm talking about. Plant knowledge is important. The Earth is rich in edible and medicinal plants.

A second source of food is a trap line of figure four dead fall traps. Their construction and use is well explained in Larry Dean Olsen's book, "Wilderness Survival Skills". Study the technique and make several with which to practice. This is a valuable survival tool and should be mastered. Setup a system of twelve to twenty traps. Almost all locations in nature have a population of small mammals. Learn to recognize their habitat. Your normal take will be rodents, mice, etc. If you don't have bait for the trap, tear the cloth from the armpit area of your shirt or t-shirt. A small piece of this material will attract the animal to the trap in search of salt or in curiosity. The trap line can be in a small area near your camp. It should yield one or two rodents a night.

When you catch a rodent, skin and clean it and then smash the meat and bones into a very fine paste. Pick out all bones that are not fully pulverized and make patties from the paste. Mix it with crushed grain seeds, such as plantain, grass, etc., or pollen from cattail plants, when available, and then cook well on or in the fire. The rodents provide a good source of protein with very little energy expended for the amount gained. The Indians made warm gloves from rodent skins. There are many sources of food in nature. Learning how to identify and use them will help you through lean times in your experiences.

The mental effect of being deprived of food can be difficult to overcome. In addition to nutrition, food satisfies many other needs. It would be wise for you to experience these effects by fasting for a day or two prior to doing it in the field out of necessity. If you fast, make sure someone knows of your intentions. Remember, you can survive for a long period of time without food. Conserve energy and use your head and you will be okay.

In severe weather you must have shelter. Good shelter should be a consideration in selecting a campsite. Often, natural shelters are at hand such as caves, rock overhangs and nests under trees. These areas can be used and improved upon with less energy expended. In selecting a shelter or shelter site, look for an area that gets good Sun, out where you can be seen, away from wind and weather, and, most important, close to the best source of materials you will require. Fuel, water and food should be as close to the shelter site as possible.

If you cannot find natural shelter, the simplest and often most effective one you can create is a wickiup. The framework is made of four, five foot sticks or logs. Place them in a pyramid or cone fashion.

Tie the main braces together at the top with nylon cord, if available, or other suitable materials at hand. Spread the base about four feet wide. Keep it just large enough to curl up within. This will conserve energy in the construction as well as in staying dry and warm. Build up the cone with many more sticks. Leave an opening facing the morning sun as well as the site of your fire pit. Cover the outside of the cone with a build up of thatch, foliage, grass or other materials. Make it thick like a haystack.

If you have plastic, place it over your built up cone. Place rocks or logs on the corners so the plastic will be anchored down in a wind. This will make it wind and water proof. If you don't have plastic or other covering such as rain gear, make sure the outside, built up of thatch, is thick or it will not shed water. You can also use earth to build up the outside. This will give you substantial insulation from the elements. Place your fire pit within three feet of the shelter entrance. You can build a heat reflector of rocks or logs behind the fire on the side away from the shelter; it will keep the inside warm and snug heat rocks in or by the fire. If conditions permit, dig out the dirt inside the shelter and place the heated rocks in the shallow pit. Cover them with dirt then fill the bottom of the shelter with any dry vegetation that will provide insulation (leaves or conifer boughs work well however, the conifer boughs will produce steam which will dampen you if not insulated). The addition or deletion to the insulation can serve as a thermostat control. If you have space blankets, use one to cover the insulation. Place the other one over you. The small round shape of the shelter will force you to sleep or rest in a fetal position which is the most effective for retaining body heat. There have been nights when I did not have a shelter constructed so I simply curled myself around a warmed stone to keep warm. In winter, snow trenches or caves can be effective shelters.

I have given you some basic techniques for physical survival. You must understand your priorities and move quickly to obtain them. I consider shelter and fire first priority, however water is also a major priority and food is last. Learn and practice the skills you will require before you are called upon to use them in an emergency. Preparation is your best ally in survival.

There are other survival needs that may be even more important than physical requirements. There are some basic psychological and philosophical concepts that are common to all successful survival experiences. These concepts appear in all situations where persons have survived conditions and circumstances that seemed insurmountable.

These **SEVEN SURVIVAL CONCEPTS** are not only useful in a emergency survival situation, but also valuable in working through many problems in daily life. The first two of these concepts have been discussed; **HONESTY** and **PERSONAL RESPONSIBILITY FOR YOUR LIFE**. I discovered the high level of interest given these concepts while training Army personnel. Most of our nightly campfire sessions focused on these concepts. Many of the pilots told me that the most meaningful and useful information given in the course was the understanding of these basic principles. As I have discussed, the first of these concepts is **HONESTY**. All too often we will not admit we have a problem or we try to cover up the problem with a lie. The worse lies are the lies we tell ourselves. The sooner we acknowledge we have a problem, the sooner corrective action can be accomplished. To do otherwise wastes precious time and energy. This concept has a strong bearing on all our lives. We all feel we are honest but, in reality, we often create illusions and rationalizations which are not in harmony with what we know to be the truth. Sometimes we live our lives by another persons value system or expectations yet all the while we carry resentment, guilt or a feeling of helplessness. Even socially accepted "white lies" do nothing but postpone what must be confronted and ultimately dealt with. The result is that we waste energy and undermine our self confidence. Without **HONESTY**, there is no foundation upon which to build a solid life. Be as honest with yourself as you can and let that honesty permeate all aspects of life. You will be amazed at how problems will be solved and eventually disappear.

The second concept is that you are **PERSONALLY RESPONSIBLE FOR THE LIFE WHICH YOU CREATE**. No one is responsible for the conduct of your life but you. We tend to give our individual power to others or institutions in exchange for promised security. This is an illusion. True security comes from discovering ones own abilities and strengths. You must live your own life and take full personal responsibility for it.

The third concept is the acknowledgment and realization that **YOUR TRUTHS AND STRENGTHS COME FROM A UNIVERSAL POWER** accessible to all of us. Your concept of this power is your own decision. Many call it God. Without exception, I have never met a person who went through an intense survival experience or severe life and death problem who did not acknowledge or rediscover that source of help and comfort. The power is real. Recognize this truth and call freely upon that source.

The fourth concept is **PRAYER**. Communication in acknowledgment and giving thanks for our individual abilities, strengths and opportunities. There is an old saying in the Army: "There are no atheists in foxholes". In a survival situation, you may find yourself really alone for the first time. You will experience an overwhelming need and urge to communicate with this source of power giving thanks for what you have and asking for what you need and hope to achieve.

The fifth concept is to be still and **LISTEN TO YOUR INNER VOICE**. In other words, you should sit, be still, and think. In a stressful or panic situation, the most important task you must accomplish is gaining self control. Sit down on the ground and breath deeply and slowly. Allow your mind to clear and your body to calm. Listen to your thoughts and they will give you the answers required. In a more relaxed and calm frame of mine, it will become much easier to make clear evaluations of your problems and sound judgments needed to take the most appropriate actions.

The sixth concept is to **LIVE IN THE PRESENT**. Worrying about past mistakes, bad predicament or anticipating problems in the future can be a tremendous waste of energy. It can also weaken the focus and concentration necessary to deal with the present situation. This concept is particularly relevant in a survival situation or emergency. Live in the present and take care of today. It conserves energy, and survival depends on the conservation of energy. Your actions each day will dictate the outcome with which you must live or die tomorrow.

The last of these seven survival concepts is to **BE POSITIVE** in your thoughts, feelings and actions. Approach life with a positive attitude and attend to any task with which you are confronted, striving for excellence and doing the best job possible. Keep your tools and equipment clean and in good repair. How you maintain them reflects your overall attitude. Be positive; it will get you through some rough times.

There is a Native American proverb that states, "The Great Spirit will never give us more than we are equipped to deal with". I am sure we all feel sometimes we have more problems than we can handle; however, remember you can make it. Its a matter of how and what you think and do.

I have a friend, Bill Chisholm, who is one of the best survival guides in North America. He has guided and worked as a firefighter and helicopter crew chief for the Bureau of Land Management, as well as an emergency trouble shooter on major disasters for the federal government. He has some thoughts he calls his "Chisholms". Think about these points when you are in a tight situation:

1.	There is no such thing as an emergency, only periods of intensified stimulation.

2.	Keep your sense of humor. Look for the light side of every problem. It can save your life.

3.	Keep a proper perspective on things. We all tend to get so close to our problems that we can't see beyond them. Step back and take time to think. The solution is there if you don't let the problem overwhelm you.

4.	The best survival tool you have is your own mind. Be creative and make adaptations that will save your life.

Remember these key thoughts when you find yourself with a problem either at work or at home, or at the intense moment when you find that you must take action to survive an emergency. Use them as a checklist for your mind just as a pilot uses a checklist to pre-flight an airplane.

- Am I being honest?
- Am I living and acknowledging personal responsibility for my life?
- Am I connected with God or whatever power I see as supreme?
- Am I taking time to communicate with this source? Prayer?
- Am I giving myself the chance to slow down and think clearly? Meditation?
- Am I living in the present rather than wasting energy by worrying about the past or trying to live in the future?
- Am I approaching life with a positive attitude?

If you can answer yes" to this checklist, the odds are that you will find solutions to your problems and survive any emergency that may challenge you.

www.ingramcontent.com/pod-product-compliance
Lightning Source LLC
Chambersburg PA
CBHW071005290526
45795CB00005B/1784